THE MINIATURE BOOK OF
CHOCOLATE

CRESCENT BOOKS
New York

Published by Salamander Books Ltd.,
129-137 York Way, London N7 9LG, United Kingdom.

© Salamander Books Ltd., 1991

All correspondence concerning the content of this volume
should be addressed to Salamander Books Ltd.

This 1991 edition published by Crescent Books, distributed by
Outlet Book Company, Inc., a Random House Company,
225 Park Avenue South, New York, New York 10003.

Printed and bound in Belgium

ISBN 0-517-06540-1

8 7 6 5 4 3 2 1

CREDITS

RECIPES BY: *Carole Handslip, Lesley Mackley, Janice Murfitt, Cecilia
Norman, Sally Taylor and Carol Timperley*

PHOTOGRAPHY BY: *Sue Atkinson, David Gill, Paul Grater and Graham
Tann*

DESIGN BY: *Tim Scott*

TYPESET BY: *Maron Graphics, Wembley*

COLOR SEPARATION BY: *P & W Graphics, Pte. Ltd.*

PRINTED IN BELGIUM BY: *Proost International Book Production,
Turnhout, Belgium*

CONTENTS

CHOCOLATE & MINT MOUSSE

6 oz semisweet chocolate, chopped
1¼ cups whipping cream
1 egg
pinch of salt
few drops peppermint extract
DECORATION:
1 small egg white
mint leaves
superfine sugar
coarsely grated semisweet chocolate to decorate

*P*ut chocolate into a food processor, or blender. In a small saucepan, bring cream almost to a boil, pour onto chocolate and process 1 minute. Add egg, salt and peppermint extract and blend 1 minute more. Pour into 1 large, or 4-6 individual, serving dishes. Refrigerate several hours.

For the decoration, in a shallow bowl, lightly whip egg white. Dip mint leaves into egg white, allow excess to drain off, then dip in the sugar to coat evenly and lightly; shake excess off. Let leaves stand on waxed paper until dried. Decorate top of mousse with grated chocolate and the mint leaves. *Makes 4-6 servings*

$\mathcal{S}$TUFFED
CHOCOLATE PEARS

2 oz amaretti cookies (macaroons), crushed
3 to 4 tablespoons Cointreau
4 oz semisweet chocolate, chopped
1 tablespoon orange juice
3 tablespoons strong coffee
2 tablespoons butter
2 eggs, separated
4 ripe medium-size pears
Orange peel curls and fresh mint to decorate, if desired

*I*n a small bowl, soak amaretti cookies in Cointreau. In a double boiler, or a bowl set over a pan of simmering water, melt chocolate in orange juice and coffee, stirring until smooth. Remove from heat and beat in butter and egg yolks. In another bowl, whip egg whites until stiff. Fold in chocolate mixture. Peel pears, leaving stems in place. Working from the bottom of each pear, carefully scoop out the core. Fill the cavity with the amaretti mixture. Set the pears upright on a wire rack, cutting off a thin slice, if necessary, to make them stand upright. Spoon melted chocolate over pears to coat evenly. Refrigerate several hours. Serve garnished with orange peel and mint, if desired. *Makes 4 servings*

$\mathscr{W}$HITE & DARK
CHOCOLATE MOUSSES

4 (1-oz) squares white chocolate, chopped
4 (1-oz) squares semisweet chocolate, chopped
1 tablespoon Cointreau
1 tablespoon dark rum
4 eggs separated
orange peel spirals to decorate

*P*lace the chocolates in separate small bowls. Add Cointreau to white chocolate, rum to dark chocolate. Place bowls over separate pans of simmering water and heat gently, stirring frequently, until smooth. Remove from heat and stir 2 egg yolks into each bowl. In a separate bowl, whip egg whites until stiff. Gently fold into each chocolate mixture until just evenly mixed. Fill 8 individual small dessert dishes with alternate spoonfuls. Let stand in a cool place until set. Decorate with orange peel spirals. *Makes 8 servings*

CHOCOLATE SOUFFLÉ

4 oz semisweet chocolate, chopped
2 tablespoons brandy or coffee
4 eggs, separated, plus 2 extra whites
1 tablespoon superfine sugar
1 recipe Dark Chocolate Sauce, page 17
TO SERVE:
powdered sugar, if desired, to decorate

*I*n the top of a double boiler, or bowl set over a saucepan of simmering water, melt chocolate in brandy or coffee, stirring frequently. Remove from heat and beat in egg yolks and sugar. In a separate bowl, whip egg whites until stiff. Stir 1 tablespoon into chocolate, then, using a metal spoon, gently fold chocolate into egg whites, until just evenly mixed. Pour into a buttered 4-cup soufflé dish, dusted inside with superfine sugar. Place on a baking sheet and bake in an oven preheated to 400F (205C) until risen and just set, about 15-18 minutes. Decorate top with a dusting of powdered sugar; serve with Dark Chocolate Sauce if desired. *Makes 4 servings*

$\mathcal{D}$ARK CHOCOLATE SAUCE

6 oz semisweet chocolate, chopped
½ cup strong coffee or water
¼ cup superfine sugar

*I*n the top of a double boiler, or bowl set over a saucepan of simmering water, melt chocolate and sugar in coffee or water, stirring frequently, until evenly mixed. Serve hot or cold. *Makes 4-6 servings*

NOTE: Serve with Chocolate Soufflé, page 14 or Chocolate Ice Cream, page 18, if desired.

VARIATIONS: Add a few drops of vanilla essence or 1 or 2 tablespoons brandy or rum. Add the flavoring gradually, beating constantly to avoid curdling.

CHOCOLATE
ICE CREAM

2 eggs plus 2 yolks
½ cup sugar
1¼ cups half and half
8 oz semisweet chocolate, chopped
1¼ cups whipping cream
¼ cup dark rum

*I*n a large bowl, combine eggs, yolks and sugar. In a large saucepan, gently heat half and half and chocolate until chocolate is melted. Stir to smooth, then bring to a boil, stirring. Stir onto egg mixture, then pour into top of a double boiler or a bowl set over a pan of boiling water. Cook, stirring constantly, until custard is thick enough to coat back of spoon. Strain into a bowl and cool. In a large bowl, whip whipping cream and rum until stiff, then fold into chocolate mixture. Pour into a freezerproof container. Cover, seal and freeze until firm 4 hours. To serve, scoop into chilled serving dishes. *Makes 6 to 8 servings*

CHOCOLATE
PROFITEROLES

CHOUX PASTRY:
4 tablespoons butter, cut in small pieces
⅔ cup water
½ cup plus 2 tablespoons all-purpose flour, sifted
2 eggs, beaten
1¼ cups whipping cream, whipped
1 recipe Dark Chocolate Sauce, page 17

*F*or the choux pastry, put butter and water into a saucepan and heat gently until butter melts. Bring to a boil and remove from heat. Beat in flour with a wooden spoon until mixture leaves sides of pan. Beat in eggs gradually, until mixture is smooth and shiny. Using a pastry bag fitted with a plain nozzle, pipe walnut-size balls onto baking sheets lined with parchment paper. Bake in an oven preheated to 400F (205C) until brown, risen and crisp, 20 to 25 minutes. Make a small hole in side of each profiterole to allow steam to escape and keep profiterole crisp. Cool on a wire rack. To serve, enlarge hole in side of each profiterole and, using a pastry bag fitted with a plain nozzle, pipe cream into them. Pour hot sauce over profiteroles. *Makes 4 servings*

CHOCOLATE
FONDUE

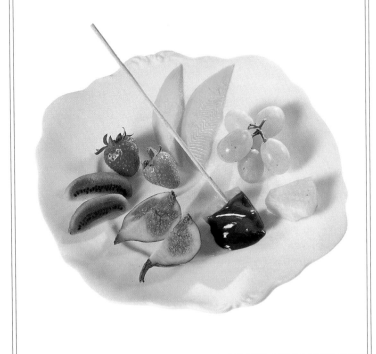

1 pineapple
1 mango
2 kiwifruit
1¾ cups strawberries
8 oz seedless green grapes
2 or 3 figs
FONDUE:
8 oz semisweet chocolate, broken in pieces
⅔ cup whipping cream
2 tablespoons brandy

*P*eel and core pineapple; cut in cubes. Peel and slice mango. Peel kiwifruit and cut in wedges. Cut figs in quarters. Arrange all fruit on 6 individual plates and leave to chill.

For the fondue, in a fondue pot, place chocolate and whipping cream. Gently heat, stirring constantly, until chocolate has melted. Stir in brandy; beat until smooth.

Keep warm over a burner, and serve fondue with fresh fruit. *Makes 6 servings*

CHOCOLATE LOG

1 (14 oz) can sweetened condensed milk
3 oz semisweet chocolate, chopped
3 tablespoons butter
1 lb plain sponge cake crumbs
½ cup walnuts, chopped
3 tablespoons chopped pitted dates
⅔ cup glacé cherries, halved
3 tablespoons butter
¼ cup superfine sugar
2 tablespoons water
½ cup powdered sugar
¼ cup unsweetened cocoa powder

*I*n a saucepan over a low heat, melt the chocolate and butter in the milk, mix evenly. Remove from heat. Stir cake crumbs into chocolate with walnuts, dates and cherries. Spoon onto a large sheet of waxed paper. Form into a roll. Roll up in the paper. Refrigerate overnight. Two hours before serving, unwrap roll and place on serving dish. For the icing, in a saucepan combine butter, superfine sugar and water. Bring to a boil. Sift powdered sugar and cocoa powder into pan and beat well. Cool and spread over roll. Decorate with glacé cherry strips and walnut halves. *Makes 8-10 servings*

$\mathscr{C}$HOCOLATE WAFFLES

4 tablespoons butter, chopped
2 oz semisweet chocolate, chopped
1½ cups all-purpose flour
1 tablespoon baking powder
1 tablespoon plus 2 teaspoons sugar
2 eggs, separated
1¼ cups milk
melted butter
chocolate-dipped strawberries, whipped cream
and ground cinnamon, to serve

*I*n the top of a double boiler, or bowl set over a saucepan of simmering water, melt chocolate and butter, stirring frequently until smooth. Sift flour and baking powder into a large bowl. Stir in sugar and make a well in the center. Add egg yolks and stir ingredients together, gradually adding the milk. Beat in melted chocolate and butter. In a bowl, whip egg whites until stiff. Gently fold into chocolate mixture. Brush a waffle iron with melted butter; heat to medium. Fill 1 half of waffle iron with mixture. Close iron and cook until steam ceases to escape, and waffles are crisp and golden, about 1 minute each side. Serve hot, with chocolate-dipped strawberries, whipped cream and cinnamon. *Makes about 10 waffles*

CHOCOLATE TRUFFLE CHEESECAKE

12 to 14 ladyfingers
2 tablespoons brandy or rum
1 (8 oz) pkg cream cheese, softened
1 cup whipping cream
1 teaspoon vanilla extract
12 oz semisweet chocolate, melted
2 egg whites, stiffly whisked

TO DECORATE:

rose leaves
2 oz milk chocolate, melted
2 oz white chocolate, melted
1 teaspoon cocoa powder

*I*n a medium-size bowl, beat together cream cheese and cream until thick. Stir in vanilla and chocolate until evenly mixed. Fold egg whites into chocolate mixture, spoon into prepared pan and level the top. Cover and refrigerate overnight. For the decoration, using a fine paint-brush, brush underside of rose leaves with milk and white chocolate. Set, chocolate side up on waxed paper; set aside to dry. Apply a second coat; let dry. Carefully peel away leaves from paper. Turn cake, upside down, onto serving plate. Dust cocoa powder around top edge and decorate top with chocolate leaves. *Makes 8-10 servings*

$\mathcal{M}$OCHA BRANDY PIE

1 (9-inch) pastry pie shell
1½ (¼ oz) pkgs. unflavored gelatin (4½ teaspoons)
⅔ cup double strength hot coffee
3 eggs, separated
¼ cup superfine sugar
3 tablespoons brandy
2 tablespoons crème de cacao
⅔ cup whipping cream, lightly whipped
2 (2-oz) squares semisweet chocolate, melted

or the *Mocha Brandy Filling*, in a small bowl, dissolve gelatin in the hot coffee. In a separate bowl, whisk together egg yolks and sugar until light. Stir in the gelatin mixture, brandy and crème de cacao. Fold in cream. In another bowl, whip egg whites until stiff. Gently fold into coffee mixture. Turn into pie shell. Refrigerate 2 to 3 hours. For the chocolate curls, pour the chocolate onto a flat, firm surface. Let stand until set. Holding a knife blade at a 45° angle, push it along the chocolate surface to form curls. Transfer to pie. *Makes 8 servings*

CHOCOLATE
CHRISTMAS PUDDING

⅓ cup glacé pineapple, coarsely chopped
⅓ cup chopped glacé cherries
⅓ cup raisins
peel of ½ orange, if desired
3 tablespoons brandy
3 tablespoons half and half
12 oz semisweet chocolate, chopped
½ cup cream cheese, softened
4 oz ratafia cookies (macaroons), broken in pieces
whipped cream and grated semisweet chocolate to serve

*I*n a small bowl, combine pineapple, cherries, raisins, orange peel and brandy. In a medium-size saucepan over very low heat, melt chocolate in half and half, stirring until smooth. Add fruit and brandy; cool. In a large bowl, beat cream cheese with 2 spoonsful chocolate mixture, then beat in remaining chocolate mixture. Add cookies and pour into a greased 3¾ cup pudding bowl. Refrigerate overnight. Turn out pudding onto a serving plate. Spoon some whipped cream over top of pudding so it trickles down the sides, and sprinkle pudding with grated chocolate; serve remaining cream separately.
Makes 10-12 servings

$\mathcal{M}$OCHA RUM TORTE

3 eggs
½ cup plus 1 tablespoon superfine sugar
¾ cup all-purpose flour
1 tablespoon instant coffee granules
12 oz mascarpone cheese
4 egg yolks
½ cup superfine sugar
2 tablespoons rum
2 egg whites, stiffly whisked
¾ cup coffee
2 (1 oz) squares semisweet chocolate, grated

*F*or the cake, in a bowl, beat eggs and sugar until thick and light. Gently fold in flour and coffee granules. Spoon into deep 8-inch round lined cake pan and bake in an oven preheated to 350F (175C) until golden, 30 minutes. Cool on a wire rack. In a bowl, beat mascarpone until soft. In another bowl, beat egg yolks and sugar until light. Stir in mascarpone and rum. Fold egg whites into cheese mixture. Cut cake horizontally in 3 layers. Put 1 layer on a plate. Sprinkle with ⅓ of coffee. Cover with ⅓ of filling. Repeat layers, finishing with cheese mixture. Refrigerate overnight. To serve, sprinkle with grated chocolate. *Makes 8 servings*

$\mathcal{M}$OCHA BROWNIES

4 (1 oz) squares semisweet chocolate, chopped
¼ cup unsalted butter, chopped
1 cup dark-brown sugar
2 eggs
1 tablespoon instant coffee granules dissolved in 1 tablespoon hot water
¾ cup all-purpose flour
½ teaspoon baking powder
pinch of salt
½ cup walnuts, chopped

*I*n a saucepan over a low heat, melt chocolate and butter. Cool. In a bowl, beat sugar and eggs until light. Fold in chocolate mixture and cooled coffee until evenly mixed. Sift flour, baking powder and salt over the surface, then lightly fold in with the nuts. Pour into a deep 8-inch square cake pan lined with waxed paper. Bake in an oven preheated to 350F (175C) until firm, about 25-30 minutes. Cool in pan 30 minutes. Serve cut into squares.
Makes 16 squares

$\mathcal{P}$AINS AU CHOCOLAT

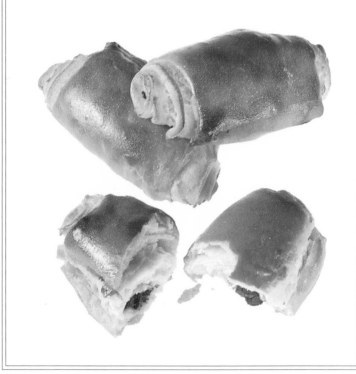

2 cups bread flour
1/4 oz pkg fast-rising yeast (2 teaspoons)
3/4 cup milk
1 tablespoon plus 2 teaspoons sugar
1 tablespoon vegetable oil
7 tablespoons butter
1/2 cup semisweet chocolate pieces (3 oz)
1 egg yolk
1 tablespoon plus 1 teaspoon milk

Sift flour into a large bowl; stir in yeast. Make a well in the center. In a small saucepan, gently heat milk, oil and sugar, stirring until sugar dissolves; cool. Stir into flour to make a smooth dough, knead lightly. Place in bowl, cover and let rise, about 2 to 3 hours. Repeat method, then let rise, about 1½ hours. Knead, then roll to a long rectangle. Dot 1/3rd of butter over top 2/3rds of dough, leaving ½-inch border. Fold lower 1/3rd up and top1/3rd down; seal edges. Repeat process twice. Fold dough in ½, cover and refrigerate 1 hour. Halve dough. Roll each piece to a rectangle 12 × 6-inch; cut in four. Sprinkle chocolate pieces in a line along width. Roll up. Place seam side down on a buttered baking sheet. Glaze, then bake at 425F (220C), about 15 to 20 minutes. *Makes 8 rolls*

CHOCOLATE CREAMS

3 oz ready-to-roll fondant icing (sugar paste)
rose and violet flavorings
pink and violet food colorings
2 oz white marzipan
6 Brazil nuts, toasted
6 whole almonds, toasted
6 (1 oz) squares semisweet chocolate, melted
6 (1 oz) squares white chocolate, melted
6 (1 oz) squares milk chocolate, melted
6 maraschino cherries
6 crème de menthe cherries
crystallized rose and violet petals

*C*ut fondant in ½, Flavor 1 piece rose, and color pink; flavor other piece violet and color pale mauve. Roll out each piece to ½-inch thick. Cut in fancy shapes; place on waxed paper. Roll small pieces of marzipan to balls, logs or ovals; place on waxed paper. Let dry several hours. Using a fork, dip 1 center at a time into 1 type of chocolate; allow excess chocolate to drain off. Place on waxed paper-lined baking sheets. Whilst wet, decorate with crystallized rose or violet petals, as appropriate, or mark with a fork or leave plain. Using a pastry bag, pipe strands of chocolate over plain shapes. *Makes 30 pieces*

CHOCOLATE TRUFFLES IN CHOCOLATE CUPS

8 (1 oz) squares semisweet chocolate, chopped
2 egg yolks
2 tablespoons unsalted butter
2 teaspoons Tia Maria
2 tablespoons whipping cream
2 teaspoons instant coffee granules
COATING:
3 (1 oz) squares semisweet or white chocolate, melted

*I*n a small bowl set over a saucepan of simmering water, melt chocolate in rum and cream, stirring until smooth. Stir in butter and coffee granules. When evenly blended, remove from heat and stir in egg yolks. Refrigerate until firm enough to handle. Roll teaspoonsful of mixture into small balls. Dip in melted chocolate, to coat; use a palette knife to roughen the surface. Let stand on a wire rack until set. Store in refrigerator; eat within 2 to 3 days. *Makes 14-16 pieces*

CHOCOLATE SYRUP

1¼ cups sugar
1¼ cups water
¾ cup unsweetened cocoa powder
TO SERVE:
milk
vanilla ice cream
whipped cream
sifted unsweetened cocoa powder

 *I*n a small saucepan, gently heat the sugar in the water, stirring until dissolved. Bring to boil; boil 3 minutes. Over moderate heat, whisk in cocoa until smooth; cool. Store in refrigerator. To serve, whisk 3 tablespoons syrup into 1 cup milk, pour into a chilled glass and top with generous dollop of whipped cream; sprinkle with cocoa powder and drink immediately. *Makes 2 cups syrup*

VARIATION: Add a teaspoon of brandy or rum at the whisking stage.